Contents

INTRODUCTION ....

CHAPTER ONE 7

Indian Cooking Basics 7

Important Techniques 7

Steaming (Dum) 8

Tempering (Baghar or Tadka) 9

Sautéing (Bhunao) 10

Grilling (Tandoori Cooking) 11

Deep-Frying (Talina) 11

Essential Ingredients 12

How to Cook with Spices 15

How to Prepare Spices 17

Basic Spices 19

How to Grind and Store Spices 20

Tools 21

CHAPTER TWO 28

INDIAN SLOW COOKER RECIPES 28

LENTIL RECIPES 30

Spiced Coconut Lentils 30

Healthy Lentil Curry 32

Delicious Black Lentil Curry 34

Lentil Butternut Squash Curry 35

BEANS AND PEAS RECIPES 36

    Healthy Chickpeas and Tofu............................37

    Chickpea Pumpkin Lentil Curry 38

    North Indian red Beans...............................40

    Simple Black-Eyed Peas.................................41

VEGETABLE RECIPES....................................43

    Delicious Spiced Potatoes and Cauliflower..............43

    Scrumptious Spinach Paneer 44

    Tasty Spinach Potato...................................45

    Spicy Eggplant Potatoes................................46

    Healthy Vegetable Coconut Curry...........................48

    Easy Whole Cauliflower Curry....................49

    Vegetable Curried Rice...............................50

    Curried Zucchini Eggplant 52

    Flavorful Vegetable Korma 53

    Potato Okra Curry 54

MEAT RECIPES..56

    Tasty Chicken Tikka Masala 56

    Delicious Chicken Tandoori..........................58

    Peanut Butter Chicken 59

    Spicy Chicken Curry....................................60

    Juicy and Tender Goat Curry.......................62

    Delicious Slow Cooked Beef........................64

    Simple Beef Curry.......................................66

Easy Curried Chicken...68

Chicken Vegetable Curry...69

INTRODUCTION

As one of the oldest civilizations still in existence, India contains over a billion people. They are spread out over a diverse set of regions, religions, languages, and even clothing choices. However, this mixture comes together to create the whole of India. Just as the country is varied, so is the food that you can find in the country. Sometimes it's defined by the region as there are some different crops that you will find it specific spots. Sometimes it will depend on the major religion of the area. People that have been in India have also changed the food that they eat as well.

Indian cuisine is loved around the world because of the variety of spices that it uses. Of course, the cuisine is still changing and evolving. The food has become more and more popular which means that the flavors aren't as foreign as they were once before. Dishes like Garam Masala and Haldi are making appearances in kitchens everywhere.

But even as people are falling in love with Indian food, people are running into another issue: time. These dishes are harder to prepare when you are up against the fast-moving pace of the rest of your life. People want to still make good food for their family, but it has to be able to work with their life. Many dishes require much more time and attention than we have to give to the dishes we want to make.

In order to help you, we're going to focus on the Dum pukht method of cooking. It is a slow cooking process. It means that you'll be cooking some food in its own juices. It uses fewer spices but keeps the flavors interesting. And these are dishes that you'll be able to put together and then go off and do everything that you need to do. You'll come home to a house that not only smells great but has a dish ready for you already.

CHAPTER ONE

Indian Cooking Basics

Everything about an Indian kitchen is wonderful. The spices and sweetness that mix there are incredibly unique and powerful in the modern world. Just the aroma of the spices will make your mouth water. The dish will be even better than the smell. Because of all the flavors and how they mix together, a lot of people have fallen in love with Indian cuisine. While some dishes might seem like they're beyond you, the dishes we are going to go over in this book are going to be well within the range of things that you can do.

Important Techniques

While the common perception is that Indian cuisine and the associated cooking styles are complicated, you'll find that there are some very not complicated techniques that will allow you to get to those complicated flavors. However, regardless of the complicated nature of the dish, there are some basics that you will need to know.

This recipe book is focused on the slow cooker recipes that you are going to be using, but there are still techniques that are going to be important to you. We're breaking them down here because you might face several of the techniques together for the same dish. It can seem intimidating when you're looking at the dish, which is why we're going to go over the basics right now and set you up for future delicious dishes.

Steaming (Dum)

Dum is the name of the technique of cooking a dish in its own steams. In cooking with a slow cooker, you will often be using a variation of this technique. This is accomplished in a slow cooker by putting the lid on top of the slow cooker and allowing none of the steam to really escape.

Dum allows the dish to keep the smell and flavors sealed inside. In the past, they would use wheat flour dough to seal the container and then set the pot on hot coals. There, the dish would cook until it was completed. Obviously, you won't be using the wheat flour dough with our recipes, but it is really interesting to know how the style of cooking was originally done.

Tempering (Baghar or Tadka)

When you use tempering, you're going to seasoning your dish with a hot oil that has spices already in it. This kind of seasoning can happen at the beginning of a recipe or towards the end. It will depend entirely on the dish.

In order to infuse the oil, you will heat the oil until it begins almost smoking. At that point, you'll turn the heat way down, then add the spices. After this, you put the oil in the dish.

There is a little bit of danger that you will need to keep in mind when you are doing this dish. When you add the ingredients to the oil, it is likely that oil will bubble and fly around you. You will need to move quickly and make sure that you are protected from the oil that might splash on you. You'll also want to avoid adding water to this mixture as it will cause the oil to splash and will reduce the flavors of the dish.

Add the ingredients to the oil one at a time to make sure that you're getting the most out of each ingredient. You should work from whole spices to the herbs to the powders.

Sautéing (Bhunao)

This is one of the most common ways of cooking foods in all of Indian cooking. You will sauté the ingredients over medium to high heat. You'll have to constantly stir the ingredients while you are going. When you are doing this, you might want to add some water to the ingredients. This will keep them from sticking to the pan while you are cooking them.

This sautéing technique will bring out the best flavors of the ingredients. But you might be uncertain about how long you need to sauté things, but you should sauté the ingredients until the fat separates from the mixture that you are cooking.

Grilling (Tandoori Cooking)

In the past, cooking in the kitchen has been done in clay ovens which are also known as tandoors. The recipes in this book don't require you to have a tandoor. They have been adjusted to better fit with the grill or oven in your kitchen.

Tandoori cooking can also include some marinating. We have included times in our recipes to make sure that you're getting the most out of the flavors in your dish. You'll definitely want to keep the dishes marinating for as long as possible.

Deep-Frying (Talina)

Deep frying is another well-known way of making dishes in India. Typically, people will use a wok or something similar in shape and depth for the oil. In this case, you might feel more comfortable using a deep fryer. There are differing opinions about how you should treat the oil for your deep frying. Common knowledge is using new oil every time. But some people like to reuse the oil. You'll want to let the oil heat up between batches of frying things. This will make sure that everything goes according to plan. You should be using just enough oil for the things that you are trying to fry. Using too much can actually be hard.

Essential Ingredients

When it comes to Indian cooking, there are some common ingredients that you will need to be aware of. They are necessary for every dish and they might be a little bit odd for you. But once you've figured out these different flavors, you'll really be able to make each dish unique and interesting.

Spices and Spice Mixes

There are many spices that are used in Indian dishes. They are found in many forms which means that there are tons of ways to really put them together. With mixes, you'll want to create mixes of spices when you need them. You don't want to have them prepared in advance because you want to make sure that all of the spices are the best they can be. However, if you don't have the time to create the mixes, you'll be able to find premade mixes in Indian grocery stores. You'll have to be very careful with the dates on the package as you want to make sure that you are getting good spices and not old ones.

Ginger-Garlic Paste

This mixture, in particular, is very important in this recipe book. In order to help you get the most out of it, we have included a recipe here so you don't have to search for one on your own. You may also be able to find a paste already mixed in an Indian grocery store. This mixture is a little bit tricky since it can cook quickly and possibly burn. You'll want to have your eyes on it while you are cooking.

Oil

When cooking Indian dishes, you will find that ghee (clarified butter) is one of the most common cooking mediums. However, you may want to use light vegetable oil instead. Ghee can provide a unique flavor to the dishes that you are making. In other areas of India, they also use mustard oil. This particular oil is more pungent and has to be heated up to its smoking point before you use it in the cooking process.

You will not find olive oil used in traditional Indian dishes. Olive oil can cause spices to lose their flavors. As well, olive oil burns more easily and cannot often stand up to the high heat required for Indian dishes.

Souring Agents

Indian dishes require so many different flavors all in one dish. In order to get the sour flavors into a dish, you will need special things to bring in the flavor. You will find that tamarind, lime or lemon juice, tomatoes, vinegar, and sometimes yogurt can be used to make a dish have a slightly sour flavor.

Tamarind and lemon juice can replace one another. If you need a souring agent that isn't wet, you will probably use amchoor or dried mango powder in order to get that flavor.

Tenderizer

In order to tenderize meat, you will often use papaya and yogurt. In this book, we also suggest pineapple as a tenderizer instead of just those two.

Thickening Agent

In order to get the body that you need from the sauces in some dishes, you will find that yogurt, chickpea flour, nut pastes, and onions are used. They can really make a sauce thicker and more appealing.

How to Cook with Spices

Spices are a definitely important part of Indian cooking. There is a lot to know about these spices. Ancient texts will often talk about how they can help the human body, preserve dishes, and add flavor to food. The ancient Indian art of healing, known as Ayurveda, focuses in particular on how food plays into the health and well-being of individuals. The texts say that in a single meal or at least once a day, you should have sweet, salty, tangy, and hot flavors. Flavors like these can be provided by spices.

Spice Combinations

When it comes to using spices, they can provide a complex flavor to seemingly simple dishes. But you also have to know how they work together. While there is no right way to mix spices, playing with spices will allow you to find the mixes that you like the most. If you're new, then you might want to take advantage of the fact that there are premade spice mixtures in Indian grocery stores everywhere. These can also just save you some time.

But when it comes to Indian food, you will want to really pay attention to the spices.

There is a learning curve of understanding the flavors when they should be added to dishes, and the order you should add them is incredibly important.

Some of the spices need to be cooked to get the most out of their flavors. There are some spices like cloves and raw green cardamom that can be used raw and as a garnish.

How to Prepare Spices

When you are preparing your spices, you need to make sure that you're doing everything right. There are several different ways to prepare spices, so we'll make sure that you're doing everything the right way.

When using oil or ghee for cooking the spices, you will need to make sure that you're getting the oil hot before you're adding the spices. Hot oil is going to retain the flavors of the spices that you are using. If the oil is cold, then you will not get as much flavor. Ghee can be heated quite hot and it will hold the flavors of spices a little bit better than most oils.

When roasting spices, you'll want to make sure that your skillet is dry. You will also want to make sure that you've gotten the skillet hot before you start adding the spices. You'll have to be prepared to move quickly as some of the spices will heat up quickly and can burn.

Also, make sure that you're making the proper substitutions of ingredients when you're trying to substitute things. Some ingredients like coriander powder cannot be replaced by fresh coriander. If you are uncertain about what can be replaced with what, use the index and we'll help you find the right substitution. You will also find that replacing ground spices instead of whole spices is something that you can easily do. The strength of the flavor goes down when you're using the powder, but that can be good sometimes.

You will want to taste your dishes often to adjust the seasonings that you are adding. You will want to make sure that your dish isn't getting over-spiced. When you are starting out, you will struggle a little bit to understand exactly how everything works together. As you learn how the spices work, you will be able to change how you use them in each dish with ease.

Before you start cooking, you'll want to make sure that your spices are ready. Many of these recipes will require your spices to be ready to go one right after the other. So, make sure that you have them set up and ready to go for when you need them.

Finally, if you burn your spices, just toss them out. You will not want to add the burned ones because they aren't going to taste good.

Basic Spices

These are the spices that you are going to need if you are cooking a lot of Indian food.

Red chili (powder and whole) Salt

Coriander (powder and whole) Cumin seeds

Turmeric

Bay Leaves

Mustard Seeds

Cinnamon

Black peppercorns

Cloves

Black and green cardamom Mango powder

Carom seeds (also known as ajwain or ajowan) Dried fenugreek leaves Tamarind pulp

How to Grind and Store Spices

When using spices, the first thing is making sure that you are using the freshest possible ingredients. You will probably want to replace your spices once a year if you aren't using them all the time. In order to test the freshness of your ingredients, you can smell them. If the spices aren't that smelly, then the spice has probably lost the potency that it once had. This is true for spices that are on their own and it is also true for spices that are mixed.

When you are grinding spices, you can use a mortar and pestle. You can also use a coffee grinder, although you will want to have a coffee grinder that is only for the spices that you are preparing.

When storing spices, you will want to keep them in a cupboard or drawer that is far away from direct sunlight. You will also want to keep things in a glass or plastic containers. This will allow you to see how much of the spice that you have.

You will want to avoid using damp utensils when getting spices from the jar. Keeping moisture away will make sure that the ingredients are lasting as long as possible. Storing ingredients in the fridge can keep them fresher especially if you live in a particularly hot area.

Tools

When it comes to cooking, there a variety of tools that you will need. We will, of course, need a slow cooker for all of the recipes in this book, but there are many more tools that you will need.

A deep pan (preferably nonstick) Tempering pan also known as Tadke ka bartan (1-to 2-cup capacity specifically for tempering) Food processor Blender

Sieve

Spice grinder (mortar and pestle, coffee grinder, etc.)

These tools are going to be the specialty tools that you need. There are other tools that you will need, but most of them will already be in your kitchen.

Masaledani

In every Indian kitchen, there is a masaledani. It is a spice box that contains 5 or 6 of the most basic spices. You'll need these spices a lot when you are cooking. In order to help make them less intimidating, we will be going over the basics of these spices.

Turmeric (Haldi)

This is one spice that you have to have. Regardless of the area of origin, turmeric is going to make an appearance in almost all of the dishes from India. You will find that this spice is very similar to ginger, so it may even look like gingerroot when you are picking it up. Fresh turmeric has a particularly strong flavor, but it is often used in a milder, ground form. In addition to flavor, turmeric adds color to food. It is even considered the Indian equivalent of saffron.

The yellow color and mild flavor are great, but turmeric can also be used as a preservative. When you're making pickles, you might use salt and turmeric as a way of keeping them good for years after you've dried them in the sun.

This spice is used to color everything from cheese to spice mixes, yogurt to salad dressing. It can also help by reducing inflammation and being used as an antiseptic. When you have a cut or bruise, you may want to rub a paste made from turmeric on it. This mixture will help you. Turmeric and warm milk can be combined to help reduce a fever as well.

Thanks to all of the properties of turmeric, there is a special place in the kitchens and homes of Indians for this spice. It is especially important for Hindu households.

Chili Powder (Lal Mirch)

Chili probably made its way into India when Vasco da Gama, a Portuguese explorer, came to the country. The spice has made its way into many of the dishes. The climate of India actually worked well with chilis and many varieties are grown across the country. Chili powder in Indian is very similar to cayenne pepper. However, unlike other areas, the ground pepper is going to be purely the ground pepper. In other parts of the world, ground pepper is sometimes combined with salt and other spices.

These peppers are going to anywhere from orange to dark red and have quite a bit to them. If you aren't able to stomach the spices, then you might need Kashmiri lal mirch. It is the milder version of chili powder and will have some color that it can add to dishes. Some people will use Kashmiri lal mirch purely for the color that it can give to a dish. Chili powder is useful in almost all dishes as many Indian dishes tend to be on the spicy side.

Cumin (Jeera)

Cumin is another of the common spices. There are several ways that cumin is found.

You can find it whole or ground. It also comes in two different forms: black and white. Black cumin, also called royal cumin, is a little bit sweeter. It is also a little bit harder to find than white cumin.

However, cumin, in general, has a warm and earthy flavor. This makes it great for soups and stews. You'll find that when you roast cumin, you will have a good flavor to add to cheese and bread. If you have roasted and ground cumin, then you'll want to add it to raita which is a yogurt-based dip. Cumin can help with your digestion, so you'll find it in the Indian form of lemonade, jal jeera.

Asafetida (Heeng)

Asafetida is a bit strong and can smell a little bit like sulfur. This can make it hard to imagine using, but the odor is something that you will smell all over the entire plant when you are cooking. This spice isn't often found in the west, but Indians use it in many different dishes.

It has a delicious flavor when added to dishes in oil. But you'll find that it has great medicinal properties. It can help with digestive issues. It can also help with lung-related issues and diseases like bronchitis and asthma. When people were a little more superstitious, they would use this spice to keep the evil spirits away from children. There are even some beliefs that it can help with anxiety and alcoholism.

This spice is mainly used for lentil dishes. You only need a pinch and sometimes even less in oil to season a whole dish. This is quite a potent spice.

Mustard Seeds (Sarson)

Mustard is a spice that people know all around the world, but it is very common in India. People will use cooked mustard greens to powdered mustard seeds. The flavors are very common. In the western parts of the world, you'll find that most people use yellow mustard, but black mustard is much more common in India.

Mustard seeds are part of salad dressing, vegetable dishes, and curry. The oil that you can get from mustard seeds is as common as olive oil is in Italy. Mustard oil was used long before vegetable oil made its way into the market, but it isn't just used for cooking. It is also used for body massages as well. The health benefits that you get from the oil are very helpful. It is a long strong tasting, so that might take some time to get used to.

Coriander Seeds (Dhaniya)

This is the last ingredient on our list, but it isn't something that you should forget. The smells of this spice are going to make your kitchen smell amazing. Coriander is known in the US as cilantro, but it is also very common in India. It is used in many sauces and as a garnish.

The fruits of this plant have seeds that have a sweet, citrus flavor and a nutty smell to them. This is a staple in the Indian kitchen. You will be able to buy whole seeds and roast them on your own. After roasting, you will want to crush them to use in other ways. You can also make a powder and use it in curries and things. There are many different ways to use these seeds, but they will always be at home in Indian cuisine.

CHAPTER TWO

<u>INDIAN SLOW COOKER RECIPES</u>

When it comes to making a recipe work in a slow cooker, many will translate easily. You'll be cooking ingredients in a little bit of liquid for a long period of time. You'll be able to play with these recipes and make them work a slow cooker even when they weren't meant to.

But you'll find that some recipes will be a little bit more difficult. Deep frying food in a slow cooker isn't going to work as well, but braising or stewing recipes are going to work easily.

You will even be able to prepare dried beans in the slow cooker. It will involve a little bit of work since you will have to soak them overnight, but it can work really well and cost you just a little bit less than canned beans. But canned beans can save you a little bit of time in the long run.

Improvisation and Shortcuts

Don't be afraid to put your own spin on things according to your unique tastes and preferences. Every recipe looks a little different in different households, so make sure that you try to take the time to make the recipe your own.

Meat

When cooking meat in a slow cooker, you will not have your meat browned in the cooker. If you want browned meat, then you're going to need to brown it a little bit before you add it to the slow cooker. Just searing the meat or quickly sautéing it will allow it to look brown.

If you are making a stew and need a thick broth, then you can coat the meat in flour. This will not only speed up the sautéing and browning but also help thicken the sauce.

Slow cooking works well with the cheaper, leaner cuts of meat that you need to cook for longer before they become tender. If you are transposing a recipe from oven or stovetop, then you might need to pick a leaner cut of meat that will be better suited to being in the slow cooker.

Make sure that you're not overcooking thing. Poultry tends to cook quickly, so just four hours on low will be enough. Poultry will turn out better when you are using wet ingredients in the slow cooker as well as it will make sure that the lean meat will not dry out.

When you're using a slow cooker, you will save time by not having to marinate your food. The marinating process happens in the slow cooker as it takes hours and hours for the flavors to become part of the dish.

LENTIL RECIPES

Spiced Coconut Lentils

Total Time: 8 hours 20 minutes Serves: 12

Ingredients

- 3 cups yellow lentils, Soak for 10 minutes 14 oz coconut milk

- ¼ cup cilantro

- 1 tbsp fresh ginger, peeled and chopped 2 tbsp curry powder

- 2 tsp ground cumin

- 2 tsp ground turmeric

- 1 tsp chili powder

- 4 chilies, stemmed and seeded 1 large onion, chopped

- 5 garlic cloves

- ½ tsp sugar

- 28 oz can tomato, diced Kosher salt

Directions

1. Rinse lentil and drain well. Add lentil into the slow cooker.

2. Add sugar, chili powder, turmeric, cumin, curry powder, ginger, garlic, onion, and

Serrano chilies into the food processor and process until mixture becomes a paste. Add into the slow cooker.

3. Stir in tomatoes and 6 cups of water.

4. Cover slow cooker and cook on low for 8 hours.

5. Season with salt and stir well.

6. Add coconut milk and stir well.

7. Garnish with cilantro and serve.

Calories 258, Fat 8 g, Carbohydrates 33 g, Sugar 4 g, Protein 13 g, Cholesterol 0 mg

Healthy Lentil Curry

Total Time: 5 hours 10 minutes Serves: 6

Ingredients

• 1 ½ cups green lentils, rinse and drained 3 tbsp tomato paste

• 14 oz can coconut milk 3 tsp curry powder

• 1 onion, diced

- 3 garlic cloves, minced 1 yellow pepper, diced ¼ tsp pepper

- ½ tsp ground ginger

- 2 tsp garam masala

- 2 tsp sugar

- 2 ½ cups water

- 2 tbsp olive oil

- 1 tsp garlic powder

- 1 tsp cumin

- 1 ½ tsp salt

Directions

1. Add olive oil, yellow pepper, garlic, and onion into the slow cooker.

2. Add lentils into the slow cooker and stir well.

3. Add all remaining ingredients and stir well.

4. Cover and cook on low for 5 hours.

5. Stir well and serve with rice.

Calories 376, Fat 19 g, Carbohydrates 39 g, Sugar 4 g, Protein 15 g, Cholesterol 0 mg

Delicious Black Lentil Curry

Total Time: 12 hours 15 minutes Serves: 8

Ingredients

• 1 cup whole black gram lentils 3 cloves

• 1 tbsp ginger, chopped 8 garlic cloves, chopped 2 green chilies, cut lengthwise 1 tbsp coriander powder ½ tsp turmeric powder ½ cup kidney beans

• 1 bay leaf

• 1 cinnamon stick

• 3 cardamom pods

• ½ tsp chili powder

• 4 tomatoes, diced

• 1 tsp garam masala

• ¼ cup cream

- 2 tbsp butter

- Salt

Directions

1. Soak black lentils and kidney beans in water for overnight.

2. Add all ingredients except cream into the slow cooker with 4 cups water and stir well.

3. Cover and cook on low for 12 hours.

4. Stir well and lightly mash using the back of a spoon.

5. Add cream and stir well.

6. Serve and enjoy.

Calories 186, Fat 4 g, Carbohydrates 27 g, Sugar 2 g, Protein 10 g, Cholesterol 9 mg

Lentil Butternut Squash Curry

Total Time: 12 hours 15 minutes Serves: 8

Ingredients

- 2 cups red lentils

- 4 cups butternut squash, cut into cubes 2 tbsp ginger, minced 1 ½ tsp curry powder 1 tsp ground coriander 1 onion, minced

- 2 garlic cloves, minced 1 tsp garam masala

- 1 tsp turmeric

- 14 oz can coconut milk 19 oz can tomato, diced 3 cups vegetable stock 1

- Tsp ground cumin

- ½ tsp salt

Directions

1. Add all ingredients into the slow cooker and stir well.

2. Cover and cook on low for 8 hours.

3. Serve and enjoy.

Calories 329, Fat 11 g, Carbohydrates 45 g, Sugar 5 g, Protein 15 g, Cholesterol 0 mg

BEANS AND PEAS RECIPES

Healthy Chickpeas and Tofu

Total Time: 4 hours 15 minutes Serves: 6

Ingredients

- 12 oz firm tofu

- 15 oz can chickpeas, rinsed and drained 1/8 cup cilantro, chopped ½ tsp ground ginger

- 2 tsp chili powder

- 1 tbsp curry powder

- 1 tbsp garam masala

- 1 cup tomato puree

- 14 oz can coconut milk

- 4 garlic cloves, minced

- 1 medium onion, diced

- 1 tsp vegetable oil

- Pepper

- Salt

Directions

1. Rinse tofu well and pat dry with paper towel. Squeeze out all liquid from tofu and cut tofu into the pieces.

2. Heat oil in the saucepan over medium heat.

3. Add onion to the pan and sauté for 5 minutes.

4. Add garlic and cook for 1 minute.

5. Whisk in coconut milk, ginger, chili powder, curry powder, garam masala, tomato puree, pepper, and salt. Cook for 5 minutes.

6. Add chickpeas and tofu into the slow cooker.

7. Pour pan mixture into the slow cooker.

8. Cover and cook on low for 4 hours.

9. Garnish with cilantro and serve.

Calories 294, Fat 18.5 g, Carbohydrates 26.2 g, Sugar 3.3 g, Protein 10.8 g, Cholesterol 0 mg

Chickpea Pumpkin Lentil Curry

Total Time: 8 hours 40 minutes Serves: 6

Ingredients

- 15 oz can chickpeas, rinsed and drained 1 cup pumpkin puree

- 1 cup lentils, rinsed and drained 15 oz can coconut milk

- ¼ tsp ground cayenne pepper 1 tbsp curry powder

- 2 cups vegetable broth

- 2 garlic cloves, minced

- 1 medium onion, diced

- 1 tsp kosher salt

Directions

1. Add all ingredients except coconut milk into the slow cooker and stir well.

2. Cover and cook on low for 8 hours.

3. Add coconut milk and stir well. Cook for another 30 minutes.

4. Serve with rice and enjoy.

Calories 376, Fat 17 g, Carbohydrates 43.5 g, Sugar 3.1 g, Protein 15.7 g, Cholesterol 0 mg

North Indian red Beans

Total Time: 4 hours 15 minutes Serves: 4

Ingredients

• 2 cups dry red beans, soak for overnight 2 tbsp cilantro, chopped 1 cup tomato sauce

• 1 cinnamon stick

• ¼ tsp turmeric

• ¼ tsp cayenne pepper

• ¼ tsp ground coriander 1 tbsp lemon juice

• 4 garlic cloves, minced

• 1 tsp ginger, minced

• 1 medium onion, chopped

• 1 tsp cumin seeds

• 1 bay leaf

• 1 tbsp vegetable oil

• 1 ½ tsp salt

Directions

1. Heat oil in the pan over medium heat.

2. Add onion, bay leaf, and cumin seeds into the pan and cook for 5 minutes.

3. Add dry spices and lemon juice and stir for 2 minutes.

4. Add beans, cinnamon stick, tomato sauce, and salt into the slow cooker.

5. Transfer pan mixture into the slow cooker and stir well.

6. Cover and cook on high for 4 hours.

7. Using spoon lightly mash the red beans it helps to thicken the gravy.

8. Garnish with cilantro and serve.

Calories 376, Fat 4.8 g, Carbohydrates 64.1 g, Sugar 5.9 g, Protein 22.2 g, Cholesterol 0 mg

Simple Black-Eyed Peas

Total Time: 6 hours 15 minutes Serves: 6

Ingredients

- 1 lb dried black-eyed peas, soak for overnight 1 tsp ground sage

- 1/8 tsp thyme

- 1 bay leaf

- 1 garlic clove, diced 1 small onion, diced 2 cups water

- 2 cups vegetable broth ½ tsp pepper

- 1 tsp sea salt

Directions

1. Add all ingredients into the slow cooker and mix well.

2. Cover and cook on low for 6 hours.

3. Serve and enjoy.

Calories 203, Fat 0.5 g, Carbohydrates 48.8 g, Sugar 2.8 g, Protein 20.2 g, Cholesterol 0 mg

VEGETABLE RECIPES

Delicious Spiced Potatoes and Cauliflower

Total Time: 4 hours 15 minutes Serves: 8

Ingredients

- 1 large cauliflower head, cut into florets 1 large potato, peeled and diced 1 tsp fresh ginger, grated

- 2 cloves garlic, minced

- 2 jalapeno peppers, sliced

- 1 medium onion, peeled and diced 1 medium tomato, diced

- 1 tbsp cumin seeds

- 1 tsp turmeric

- 3 tbsp vegetable oil

- 1 tbsp fresh cilantro, chopped 1/4 tsp cayenne pepper

- 1 tbsp garam masala

- 1 tbsp kosher salt

Directions

1. Add all ingredients except cilantro into the slow cooker and mix well.

2. Cover and cook on low for 4 hours.

3. Garnish with cilantro and serve.

Calories 123, Fat 5.6 g, Carbohydrates 16.7 g, Sugar 4 g, Protein 3.6 g, Cholesterol 0 mg

Scrumptious Spinach Paneer

Total Time: 5 hours 15 minutes Serves: 6

Ingredients

• 12 oz paneer cheese

• 8 oz fresh spinach, chopped 30 oz frozen spinach, thawed 14 oz can coconut milk

• 1/8 tsp cayenne pepper

• 1 tbsp ground cumin

• 1 tbsp ground coriander

• 1 tbsp garam masala

- 1 ½ cups can tomato sauce 3 tbsp fresh ginger, minced 4 garlic cloves, chopped

- 1 tsp salt

Directions

1. Add all ingredients except fresh spinach and paneer into the slow cooker.

2. Cover and cook on low for 3 hours.

3. Add fresh spinach and cook for 1 hour.

4. Using immersion blender blend mixture until smooth.

5. Add paneer cheese and cook for 1 hour.

6. Serve and enjoy.

Calories 220, Fat 10 g, Carbohydrates 16 g, Sugar 6 g, Protein 20 g, Cholesterol 0 mg

Tasty Spinach Potato

Total Time: 3 hours 15 minutes Serves: 4

Ingredients

- 1 1/2 lbs potatoes, peel and cut into chunks 1/2 lb fresh spinach, chopped ½ tsp chili powder 1/2 tsp garam masala 1/2 tsp ground coriander 1/2 tsp cumin
- 1 tbsp vegetable oil 1/4 cup water
- 1/2 onion, sliced
- Pepper
- Salt

Directions

1. Add all ingredients into the slow cooker and stir well.

2. Cover and cook on low for 3 hours.

3. Serve and enjoy.

Calories 168, Fat 3.9 g, Carbohydrates 30.4 g, Sugar 2.8 g, Protein 4.7 g, Cholesterol 0 mg

Spicy Eggplant Potatoes

Total Time: 2 hours 40 minutes Serves: 8

Ingredients

- ½-inch cubes 2 jalapeño chilies, seeded and minced 1 tbsp ground cumin
- 1 tbsp chili powder
- 1 medium onion, chopped
- 1 tsp ginger, grated
- 6 garlic cloves, minced
- 1 tbsp garam masala
- 1 tsp turmeric
- 2 tbsp fresh cilantro, chopped 1/4 cup vegetable oil
- 1 tbsp kosher salt

Directions

1. Add all ingredients into the slow cooker and stir well.

2. Cover and cook on high for 2 hours.

3. Remove lid and cook on low for another 30 minutes.

4. Serve and enjoy.

Calories 147, Fat 7.5 g, Carbohydrates 19.4 g, Sugar 5.2 g, Protein 2.9 g, Cholesterol 0 mg

Healthy Vegetable Coconut Curry

Total Time: 4 hours 20 minutes Serves: 8

Ingredients

- ¼ cup cilantro, chopped 1 cup green peas

- 1 ½ cups carrots, peeled and cut into strips 14 oz can coconut milk

- 1 oz dry onion soup mix

- 2 bell pepper, cut into strips ½ tsp cayenne pepper

- ½ tsp red pepper flakes 1 tbsp chili powder

- 2 tbsp flour

- ¼ cup curry powder

- 5 potatoes, peeled and cut into cubes Water as needed

Directions

1. Add all ingredients into the slow cooker and mix well.

2. Cover and cook on low for 4 hours.

3. Stir well and serve.

Calories 370, Fat 18.3 g, Carbohydrates 48.8 g, Sugar 5.4 g, Protein 8.2 g, Cholesterol 0 mg

Easy Whole Cauliflower Curry

Total Time: 4 hours 15 minutes Serves: 4

Ingredients

• 1 large cauliflower head, trimmed 2 garlic cloves, sliced

• ½ onion, chopped

• 2 small potatoes, quartered 1 red pepper, sliced

For sauce:

• ½ tsp cayenne pepper

- 1 tsp cumin

- 2 tbsp curry powder

- 2 cups can coconut milk

- 2 cups vegetable broth

Directions

1. Add red pepper, potatoes, onion, garlic, and cauliflower into the slow cooker.

2. In a bowl, whisk together all sauce ingredients and pour over cauliflower.

3. Cover and cook on low for 4 hours.

4. About 15 minute's before serving add coconut milk and stir well.

5. Serve and enjoy.

Calories 383, Fat 25.8 g, Carbohydrates 34.3 g, Sugar 8.6 g, Protein 11.4 g, Cholesterol 0 mg

Vegetable Curried Rice

Total Time: 4 hours 10 minutes Serves: 4

Ingredients

- 1 ½ cups green cabbage, chopped 2 cups mushrooms, chopped 1 cup broccoli, chopped

- 1 cup brown rice

- 1 tsp curry powder

- 2 tbsp apple cider vinegar 1/4 tsp dried thyme

- ½ tsp garlic powder

- ½ tsp black pepper

- 4 cups vegetable broth

- 1 tsp salt

Directions

1. Add all ingredients into the slow cooker and mix well.

2. Cover and cook on low for 4 hours.

3. Using fork fluff the rice.

4. Serve and enjoy

Calories 237, Fat 2.9 g, Carbohydrates 42.1 g, Sugar 2.7 g, Protein 10.7 g, Cholesterol 0 mg

Curried Zucchini Eggplant

Total Time: 4 hours 15 minutes Serves: 4

Ingredients

• 4 cups zucchini, chopped 4 cups eggplant, peeled and chopped ¼ cup vegetable broth 15 oz can coconut milk 6 oz can tomato paste

• ¼ tsp cumin

• ¼ tsp cayenne pepper 1 tbsp garam masala

• 1 tbsp curry powder

• 4 garlic cloves, minced 1 onion, chopped

• 1 tsp salt

Directions

1. Add all ingredients into the slow cooker and mix well.

2. Cover and cook on low for 4 hours.

3. Stir well and serve with rice.

Calories 307, Fat 23.6 g, Carbohydrates 24.3 g, Sugar 10.9 g, Protein 7.2 g, Cholesterol 0 mg

Flavorful Vegetable Korma

Total Time: 5 hours 15 minutes Serves: 4

Ingredients

- 2 tbsp almond meal
- 1 tbsp red pepper flakes
- 1 tsp garam masala
- 2 tbsp curry powder
- 10 oz coconut milk
- 2 garlic cloves, minced
- ½ large onion, chopped
- 1 cup green beans, chopped ½ cup frozen green peas 2 large carrots, chopped
- 1 large cauliflower head, cut into florets 1 tsp sea salt

Directions

1. Add all ingredients into the slow cooker and stir well.

2. Cover and cook on high for 5 hours.

3. Serve and enjoy.

Calories 295, Fat 19.4 g, Carbohydrates 28.7 g, Sugar 11.8 g, Protein 9.1 g, Cholesterol 0 mg

Potato Okra Curry

Total Time: 3 hours 15 minutes Serves: 6

Ingredients

• 1 ½ lbs potatoes, peeled and cut into pieces 1 lb okra, cut the ends and sliced 2 cups vegetable stock

• 13 oz can coconut milk

• 1 ½ tbsp curry powder

• ¾ tsp red pepper flakes

• 2 tsp fresh ginger, grated

• 4 garlic cloves, minced

- 1 large onion, chopped

- 1 1/2 tbsp vegetable oil

- 1 bell pepper, seeded and chopped 1 ½ tsp salt

Directions

1. Add potatoes, bell pepper, and okra into the slow cooker.

2. Heat oil in a pan over medium heat.

3. Add garlic, onion, and ginger to the pan and sauté for 5 minutes.

4. Remove pan from heat and stir in spices.

5. Transfer pan mixture into the slow cooker and stir well.

6. Cover and cook on low for 3 hours.

7. Stir well and serve with rice.

Calories 290, Fat 17.8 g, Carbohydrates 31.8 g, Sugar 5.3 g, Protein 5.5 g, Cholesterol 0 mg

MEAT RECIPES

Tasty Chicken Tikka Masala

Total Time: 6 hours 25 minutes Serves: 6

Ingredients

- 2 lbs chicken thighs, skinless and boneless, cut into 2-inch pieces

- 10 oz frozen peas, thawed

- 1 ½ cups heavy cream

- 1 tbsp cornstarch

- 1 tbsp sugar 28 oz can tomato

- 1 tsp ginger, grated

- 3 tbsp garam masala

- ½ tsp red pepper flakes

- 6 garlic cloves, minced

- 1 large onion, diced

- 2 tbsp vegetable oil

- 1 cup plain yogurt

- 1 tbsp ground cumin

- 1 tbsp ground coriander

- 1 tsp kosher salt

Directions

1. In a large bowl, combine together chicken, yogurt, cumin, ground coriander, and salt. Marinade for 10 minutes.

2. Heat 1 tbsp oil in the pan over medium-high heat.

3. Place marinated chicken into the pan and cook until lightly brown on both the sides.

4. Transfer chicken into the slow cooker.

5. In the same pan, heat remaining oil. Add onions, red pepper flakes, and garlic and sauté for 5 minutes.

6. Add ginger, garam masala, and salt and cook for 1 minute.

7. Add sugar and tomatoes, turn heat to high and bring to boil. Transfer into the slow cooker.

8. Cover and cook on low for 6 hours.

9. Whisk together 1/4 cup heavy cream and cornstarch and add to the slow cooker along with remaining peas and heavy cream.

10. Stir to mix and cover and cook for another 10 minutes.

11. Serve and enjoy.

Calories 557, Fat 27.8 g, Carbohydrates 24.5 g, Sugar 12.7 g, Protein 51.1 g, Cholesterol 178 mg

Delicious Chicken Tandoori

Total Time: 8 hours 20 minutes Serves: 4

Ingredients

• 14 oz coconut milk

• 4 chicken thighs

• 1 tsp fresh ginger, grated 1 tsp paprika

• 1 tsp cayenne pepper

• 2 tsp tomato paste

• 2 tsp garam masala

• 1 tsp ground coriander 1 tsp ground cumin

Directions

1. Add all ingredients into the slow cooker and mix well.

2. Cover and cook on low for 8 hours.

3. Serve and enjoy.

Calories 514, Fat 34.8 g, Carbohydrates 7.1 g, Sugar 3.8 g, Protein 44.9 g, Cholesterol 130 mg

Peanut Butter Chicken

Total Time: 4 hours 30 minutes Serves: 6

Ingredients

- 3 chicken breasts, skinless and boneless 1 tbsp lime juice

- 2 tbsp cornstarch

- 3 garlic cloves, minced

- 1 tbsp ginger, minced

- 1 tbsp rice wine vinegar 2 tbsp honey

- 2 tbsp soy sauce

- 1/3 cup creamy peanut butter 1 cup coconut milk

Directions

1. Add all ingredients except lime juice and cornstarch into the slow cooker and mix well.

2. Cover and cook on low for 4 hours.

3. Whisk together cornstarch and 2 tbsp water and pour into the slow cooker.

4. Stir well and cook for another 20 minutes until gravy thickens.

5. Serve and enjoy.

Calories 356, Fat 22.2 g, Carbohydrates 15.4 g, Sugar 8.7 g, Protein 26.2 g, Cholesterol 65 mg

Spicy Chicken Curry

Total Time: 6 hours 20 minutes Serves: 4

Ingredients

- 4 chicken thighs, boneless and cut into chunks

- 3 tbsp flour

- 2 tsp ground coriander

- 2 tsp garam masala

- 2 tsp turmeric

- 2 tsp ground cumin

- 1 tsp ginger, grated

- ½ lemon juice

- 4 garlic cloves, crushed

- 2 onion, chopped

- 2 green chilies, chopped

- 14 oz can tomato, chopped

- 1 tbsp vegetable oil

Directions

1. Add ginger, chilies, garlic, and onion into the blender and blend until smooth.

2. Heat oil in the pan over medium heat.

3. Add blended puree into the pan and sauté for 3 minutes.

4. Add spices and sauté for 2-3 minutes.

5. Add flour and tomatoes into the pan and stir well.

6. Refill tomato can halfway with water and adds in the pan. Stir well.

7. Add chicken into the slow cooker and season with pepper and salt.

8. Pour pan mixture over the chicken with lemon juice.

9. Cover and cook on low for 6 hours.

10. Serve and enjoy.

Calories 387, Fat 14.8 g, Carbohydrates 17.3 g, Sugar 6 g, Protein 44.9 g, Cholesterol 130 mg

Juicy and Tender Goat Curry

Total Time: 5 hours 15 minutes Serves: 6

Ingredients

• 2 lbs goat meat

- 2 Serrano pepper, minced
- 1 tsp paprika
- 1 tsp chili powder
- 1 tsp turmeric powder
- 1 tsp cumin powder
- 1 tbsp coriander powder
- 2 cardamom pods
- 2 garlic cloves, minced
- 1 tbsp ghee
- 1 bay leaf
- 3 whole cloves
- 1 tsp fresh ginger, minced
- 1 large onion, chopped
- 1 cup water
- 1 tsp garam masala
- 28 oz can tomato, diced
- 2 tsp salt

Directions

1. Add cardamom and cloves into the grinder and grind well.

2. Add all ingredients into the slow cooker except water, garam masala, and tomatoes.

3. Cover and cook on high for 4 hours.

4. Add water, garam masala, and tomatoes and stir well.

5. Cook for another 1 hour until meat is tender.

6. Serve and enjoy.

Calories 230, Fat 5.9 g, Carbohydrates 10.6 g, Sugar 5.8 g, Protein 33.6 g, Cholesterol 92 mg

Delicious Slow Cooked Beef

Total Time: 6 hours 15 minutes Serves: 4

Ingredients

• 2 lbs beef chuck steak, diced

• ½ cup coriander, chopped

• 2 cardamom pods

- 1 cinnamon stick
- 14 oz can tomato, diced
- ¼ cup curry paste
- 1 red chili, chopped
- 1 tsp ginger, grated
- 2 garlic cloves, crushed
- 1 large onion, sliced
- 2 tbsp vegetable oil
- ¼ cup plain flour

Directions

1. Add beef and flour into the Ziplock bag and shake well.

2. Heat oil in the saucepan over medium heat.

3. Add beef into the saucepan and cook for 3-4 minutes or until lightly brown. Transfer beef into the slow cooker.

4. In the same pan, add onion, ginger, and garlic and sauté for 4 minutes.

5. Add curry paste and chili and stir for 1 minute.

6. Add ¾ cup water, tomatoes, cardamom, and cinnamon and stir well.

7. Transfer mixture into the slow cooker.

8. Cover and cook on low for 5 ½ hours or until beef is tender.

9. Add coriander and stir well.

10. Serve and enjoy.

Calories 651, Fat 29.9 g, Carbohydrates 19.7 g, Sugar 5 g, Protein 71.8 g, Cholesterol 203 mg

Simple Beef Curry

Total Time: 8 hours 40 minutes Serves: 4

Ingredients

- 12 oz beef steak, cut into 1-inch pieces
- 2 onions, chopped
- 14 oz can tomato, chopped
- 2 tsp garam masala

- 4 garlic cloves, chopped

- 4 tsp ground cumin

- 4 tsp ground coriander

- 2 tsp ground turmeric

- 2 chilies, chopped

- 1 tsp ginger, grated

- 7 oz yogurt

- 4 tbsp vegetable oil

Directions

1. Heat oil in the pan over medium heat.

2. Add beef to the pan and cook for 4-5 minutes or until lightly brown.

3. Transfer beef into the slow cooker.

4. In the same pan, sauté onion, ginger, chili, and garlic for 2 minutes.

5. Add spices and stir-fry for 1 minute. Transfer pan mixture to the slow cooker.

6. Add remaining ingredients except for yogurt into the slow cooker and stir well.

7. Cover and cook on low for 8 hours.

8. Add yogurt and stir well and cook for another 30 minutes.

9. Serve and enjoy.

Calories 375, Fat 20.2 g, Carbohydrates 16.7 g, Sugar 9.3 g, Protein 30.8 g, Cholesterol 79 mg

Easy Curried Chicken

Total Time: 4 hours 15 minutes Serves: 4

Ingredients

- 2 tbsp tomato paste

- 14 oz can coconut milk

- 3 garlic cloves, minced

- 2 tbsp fresh ginger, minced

- 1 tsp cumin

- 1 tsp turmeric

- 1 tsp garam masala

- 1 cinnamon stick

- 2 bay leaves

- 1 ½ lbs chicken thighs 1 medium onion, diced

- ¼ cup fresh cilantro, chopped 1 ½ tsp salt

Directions

1. Add all ingredients into the slow cooker and stir well.

2. Cover and cook on low for 4 hours.

3. Using fork shred the meat and stir well into the sauce.

4. Serve and enjoy.

Calories 553, Fat 34.2 g, Carbohydrates 10.2 g, Sugar 2.3 g, Protein 52.4 g, Cholesterol 151 mg

Chicken Vegetable Curry

Total Time: 3 hours 25 minutes Serves: 4

Ingredients

- 2 cups mushrooms, sliced

- 1 cup green peas

- 3 chicken breasts, skinless, boneless and cut into pieces
- 2 tsp ground cayenne
- ½ tsp black pepper
- 3 tbsp curry powder
- 1 packet dry onion soup mix
- 14 oz can coconut milk
- 10.75 oz can chicken soup
- 10.75 oz can mushroom soup
- 1 onion, chopped
- 1 tbsp butter

Directions

1. Melt butter in the pan over medium heat.

2. Add onion and cook for 5 minutes. Transfer to the slow cooker.

3. Add remaining ingredients and stir well.

4. Cover and cook on high for 1 ½ hours then reduce heat to low and cook for another 1 ½ hours.

5. Serve and enjoy.

Calories 635, Fat 37.9 g, Carbohydrates 32 g, Sugar 2.3 g, Protein 45.2 g, Cholesterol 111 mg

Printed in Great Britain
by Amazon